IT'S TIME TO EAT HAWAIIAN PIZZA

It's Time to Eat HAWAIIAN PIZZA

Walter the Educator

Silent King Books
A WhichHead Entertainment Imprint

Copyright © 2024 by Walter the Educator

All rights reserved. No part of this book may be reproduced in any manner whatsoever without written per- mission except in the case of brief quotations embodied in critical articles and reviews.

First Printing, 2024

Disclaimer

This book is a literary work; the story is not about specific persons, locations, situations, and/or circumstances unless mentioned in a historical context. Any resemblance to real persons, locations, situations, and/or circumstances is coincidental. This book is for entertainment and informational purposes only. The author and publisher offer this information without warranties expressed or implied. No matter the grounds, neither the author nor the publisher will be accountable for any losses, injuries, or other damages caused by the reader's use of this book. The use of this book acknowledges an understanding and acceptance of this disclaimer.

It's Time to Eat HAWAIIAN PIZZA is a collectible early learning book by Walter the Educator suitable for all ages belonging to Walter the Educator's Time to Eat Book Series. Collect more books at WaltertheEducator.com

USE THE EXTRA SPACE TO TAKE NOTES AND DOCUMENT YOUR MEMORIES

HAWAIIAN PIZZA

It's time to eat, it's pizza day!

It's Time to Eat Hawaiian Pizza

A special treat is on the way.

Cheese and toppings, so much fun,

Hawaiian pizza's number one!

The crust is golden, soft, and round,

The yummiest base we've ever found.

Tomato sauce, a tangy spread,

Paint it bright, a tasty red!

Pineapple chunks so juicy and sweet,

A fruity twist we get to eat!

They shine like sunshine on each slice,

Hawaiian pizza sure is nice!

Next comes ham, so smoky and thin,

Layer it gently, let's begin.

It adds a flavor, salty and fine,

This pizza's taste is so divine!

It's Time to Eat
Hawaiian Pizza

Sprinkle cheese, a melty treat,

Mozzarella makes it complete.

Into the oven, it starts to bake,

Oh, the smells it's sure to make!

The timer dings, it's ready now,

The pizza's done, let's take a bow!

Slice it up and serve it round,

The best meal ever, we have found!

Little hands reach out to try,

A cheesy bite, oh me, oh my!

The sweet and salty mix is grand,

Hawaiian pizza's in demand!

What's your favorite, crust or cheese?

Pineapple topping always will please.

Every bite's a tasty treat,

It's Time to Eat
Hawaiian Pizza

Hawaiian pizza can't be beat!

We laugh, we munch, we feel so glad,

Sharing pizza makes us less sad.

It's not just food, it's love we share,

Hawaiian pizza shows we care.

So every time it's pizza night,

Let's make Hawaiian, it's just right!

A little sweet, a little fun,

It's Time to Eat
Hawaiian Pizza

Hawaiian pizza's number one!

ABOUT THE CREATOR

Walter the Educator is one of the pseudonyms for Walter Anderson. Formally educated in Chemistry, Business, and Education, he is an educator, an author, a diverse entrepreneur, and he is the son of a disabled war veteran.
"Walter the Educator" shares his time between educating and creating. He holds interests and owns several creative projects that entertain, enlighten, enhance, and educate, hoping to inspire and motivate you. Follow, find new works, and stay up to date with Walter the Educator™

at WaltertheEducator.com

www.ingramcontent.com/pod-product-compliance
Lightning Source LLC
LaVergne TN
LVHW010623070526
838199LV00063BA/5252